The DADS' Book

The DADS' Book

FOR THE DAD WHO'S

Best AT Everything

MICHAEL HEATLEY

SCHOLASTIC INC.

New York   Toronto   London   Auckland   Sydney

Mexico City   New Delhi   Hong Kong   Buenos Aires

*The author would like to thank Nephele Headleand, Nigel Cross,
and Ian and Claire Welch for their invaluable assistance,
as well as Rod Green and everyone at Michael O'Mara Books.*

Library of Congress Cataloging-in-Publication data is available.

ISBN-13: 978-0-545-04219-2
ISBN-10: 0-545-04219-4

First published in Great Britain in 2007 by Michael O'Mara Books Limited.

Text copyright © 2007 by Michael O'Mara Books Limited
Illustrations copyright © 2007 by Michael O'Mara Books Limited
Cover design by Angie Allison

Illustrations on pages 1, 9, 10, 11, 17, 20, 21, 22, 25, 31, 34, 39, 47, 50, 51, 52, 59, 64, 66, 68, 69, 71, 79, 103, 111, 114 © David Woodroffe 2007
Illustration on page 54 from IMST's Master Clips Collection
Illustrations on pages 65, 91, 105, 108 © Jupiter Images Corporation

12 11 10 9 8 7 6 5 4 3 2 1   8 9 10 11 12 13/0

Printed in the U.S.A.
First American edition, May 2008

Disclaimer: Even the best dads need to make sure that their children are always closely supervised when engaged in any of the practical activities mentioned in this book.

Contents

CONTENTS

Introduction

Whoever said that you have to be half mad to become a dad was only half right. You have to be completely insane!

Okay, okay, not really. But fatherhood is a big adjustment from your days as a bachelor when pizza was considered the cornerstone of a balanced diet and wearing the same shirt for three days in a row was perfectly acceptable. Back in those days, life was all about you and your whims. All-night poker games with the guys? Why not! Cheeseburgers for breakfast, lunch, and dinner? Of course! A steady stream of ESPN and action flicks? Obviously!

But life's different now. It's not just you anymore, now there's someone else to consider, someone who's going to learn by the example you set. While this is a scary thought, being a father doesn't have to be. The fact that you're reading this is proof enough that you're already on the road to becoming a fine father!

So take a deep breath, think about all the fun you're going to have, and keep reading. Whether it's diaper changing (or getting out of it altogether!), building bows and arrows, or whipping up a quick meal for the family, you're on your way to becoming the dad who's best at everything!

You can tell a child is growing up when he stops asking where he came from and starts refusing to tell where he is going.
Anonymous

Your Baby's Star Sign

Getting to know your child is a joy for any dad. This astrological guide may help you get ahead of the game.

♑ Capricorn (December 22–January 19)

Inside every Capricorn child is a wise old soul with a sense of responsibility. Don't let this interfere with the natural stages of development. Encourage balance, ease, laughter, risk-taking, and realistic goal-setting. Reinforce the idea that the journey is just as important as the destination.

♒ Aquarius (January 20–February 18)

A free spirit, the young Aquarian thrives on change and surprise, not routine. Aquarians are original thinkers, so give your child space to explore and you'll be surprised by what he or she discovers. Sometimes this unique perspective can create feelings of isolation and loneliness, so your child will need your help finding his or her way socially.

♓ Pisces (February 19–March 20)

Pisces are highly sensitive children who require love, care, and closeness in order to feel safe in this world. Pisces children appreciate order, structure, and assistance in setting goals.

Gently nudge them toward greater independence and encourage communication. Be aware that your son or daughter may have fears that block progress.

Aries (March 21–April 19)

Aries children are assertive and independent, seeking new experiences. He or she will be outgoing, competitive, and excited about the world. Don't be surprised if your youngster is in a hurry to walk, so provide a safe environment where energy can be focused and potential realized. Teach the value of completing tasks and encourage sensitivity to others.

Taurus (April 20–May 20)

Your Taurus baby thrives on affection and creature comforts. Food and a loving touch play important roles in meeting this sign's primary need: to feel a consistent sense of security in the world. A serene environment with dependable routines helps your child enjoy each day. To help develop positive personality traits and fulfill innate potential, let your Taurus child explore at his or her own pace.

Gemini (May 21–June 20)

Mentally alert, responsive, and incredibly entertaining, Gemini children have a capacity for early mental and social development. Avoid overstimulating this active mind; storytelling can help your Gemini child to relax. It is typical for a Gemini child to have too many interests going on at the same time, sometimes leading to a sense of distraction that can be a handicap in school. Create an atmosphere that supports concentration and inquisitiveness, and if your Gemini child asks endless questions, show him or her how to find the answers.

Cancer (June 21–July 22)

The young Cancerian is sensitive, imaginative, and aware of others' feelings. Hold your child as much as possible, letting him or her know that you intend to create a safe place as long as need be; it'll be clear when the time comes to help your child build a separate identity and greater self-confidence. Encourage your child to take creative risks. Although he or she relies mostly on intuition, memory will play an important part in his or her success at school. Your child appreciates structure and guidelines from positive authority figures.

Leo (July 23–August 22)

Confidence and self-respect are Leo traits; with these, your child can see the potential for creative self-expression and leadership. You can cultivate these attributes by providing honest feedback, praise, and attention. Be aware that competition for attention among family members can translate into problems in future relationships, so be understanding rather than indifferent so that your young Leo doesn't have to fight for your affection.

🦈 Virgo (August 23–September 22)

Virgo children are acutely observant, bright, alert to subtle patterns, and eager to understand how everything works. Virgo kids are sensitive to criticism and attached to the idea of being right. As a parent, you should try to show acceptance and forgiveness. Virgo children require routines to feel safe and are happy to help out mom and dad around the house.

⚖ Libra (September 23–October 22)

This child is eager to please and tends to follow role models. Overly sensitive to harsh environments, your little Libra will appreciate beauty, balance, and serenity. He or she will be loving and responsive and in many cases will assume the role of the peacemaker. Librans have a natural inclination toward theater, music, art, romance, and happily-ever-after stories. As they grow older, their need for beauty, balance, and fair play becomes motivation to enhance their lives and the lives of others.

There isn't a child who hasn't gone out into the brave new world who eventually doesn't return to the old homestead carrying a bundle of dirty clothes.
Art Buchwald

🦂 Scorpio (October 23–November 21)

A Scorpio is inquisitive and not easily coerced into doing what others expect. You're better off winning his or her cooperation than going head-to-head with one; a predominant characteristic of this sign is a tremendous amount of willpower. Betrayal is not quickly forgotten. The trusting child will share private feelings and will count on you to keep those secrets and respect his or her personal likes and dislikes. With such a deep connection, this child will enjoy a close parental relationship.

🏹 Sagittarius (November 22–December 21)

Your Sagittarius baby will be restless and inquisitive, filled with enthusiasm, and an inborn optimism. Keep him or her entertained with the wonder of new experiences. Once able to walk, your youngster will be out the door and around the block before you know it! Teach your child to deal with the negative as well as the positive, though he or she won't easily accept "no" and "can't." Things usually come without much effort for the Sagittarian. A sport or other activity requiring effort and self-discipline is a good foundation for future success.

*A father is someone who carries pictures in his wallet
where his money used to be.*
Anonymous

Ten Lamest Excuses

1. "With everything else you asked me to do today, I forgot."

2. "I only went for one drink, but they wouldn't let me leave."

3. "I thought you said you would do it."

4. "It was the dog."

5. "I don't know how."

6. "I would do it, but if I don't root for my team they could lose."

7. "The car broke down and when I got to the store, it was closed."

8. "I'm sorry, I never got your message."

9. "Traffic."

10. "Your mother stopped by, the kids were getting up, the microwave wasn't working, I couldn't find the can opener, the phone never stopped ringing, and the dog decided to pee on the carpet, so I just didn't get around to it."

Some people have got advice (about fatherhood), some people have got horror stories. I like people that look you in the eye with a glow and say, "It's gonna be cool."
Russell Crowe

How to Avoid Changing a Dirty Diaper

The gunk that goes into the top end of a baby is pretty disgusting, but it's got nothing on the stuff that comes out the other end. Let's make no bones about it, changing a diaper isn't in any way pleasant. But ask anyone with a child, and they will tell you, "It's different when it's your own baby." They're all liars. The only difference is that when it's your own kid's poop, you have to deal with it so often that you simply get used to it.

If you really can't bear the thought of getting stuck with the job, you need preparation and mental agility to be able to come up with a justifiable reason why your partner should take on the task . . . a task that she's probably undertaken several times already that day. Keep an eye — or more usefully a nose — on your child and, once you know the deed has been done, put your plan into action. Here are a few suggestions to get you thinking in the right mode:

1 Offer to call her mother to bring her up-to-date on the day's events. Your partner will be too stunned to

think there is an ulterior motive — just don't overuse this one!

2. If there's a job around the house that you've been getting nagged to do, start doing it. Your partner will put up with changing the diaper if it means that the spare room is redecorated or the fence is mended.

3. Make sure any other children are entertained. Either sit down with them and help with their homework, play a game, or take them to the park.

4. Don't just volunteer to do a household chore, actually get up and start doing the laundry, the dishes, or the ironing.

5. If you're really on top of your game, then you will have noticed the situation before your partner realizes what your child has done and you'll have popped out to the supermarket to do the shopping.

6. Feign serious illness.

It's all about paying attention and trying to stay one step ahead. Always be thinking of new excuses. You've got between two and three years of this before you're in the clear.

How to Change a Diaper

If all else fails, you may actually have to roll up your sleeves and change the diaper yourself. Let every whiff that scorches your nasal hair be a reminder to you to think up some more excuses for next time! In the meantime, here's how it's done.

First, always make sure to lay your baby on a flat, soft surface, ideally a waterproof changing pad. Babies should never be left unattended except in their crib, because they can roll over and fall from a high surface.

1 Wash your hands well.

2 Remove any jewelry that could scratch the baby.

3 Make sure you have everything ready to clean and change the baby.

4 Put a couple of safe toys in the baby's view or sing a nursery rhyme to soothe your child.

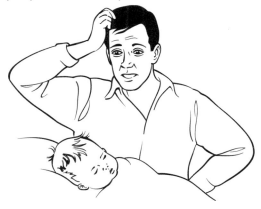

(5) Remove the dirty diaper. As you take it off, hold the baby gently by the ankles and lift the hips. Throw away the dirty diaper.

(6) Wipe the baby clean and dry well.

(7) Apply cream to prevent diaper rash.

(8) Unfold a new diaper, lift the baby's hips again, and slip it underneath.

(9) Bring the front of the diaper up between the baby's legs.

(10) Fasten the adhesive strips snugly, but not too tight.

(11) Put the baby's clothes back on.

(12) Wash your hands again.

You may find yourself all "fingers and thumbs" at first, but after a few tries, you'll become extremely good at it. And that's just as well — after all, it'll be happening at least five times a day, not counting the night changes.

The above, of course, only applies to disposable diapers. If your partner has "gone green" and decided to use cloth diapers, brush up on your evasion strategies or feign death.

What to Do While Mom's Away

If your partner has to go away for a few days on business, it may be time to start groveling to your mother-in-law and taking back all those things you said when you thought she wasn't listening. Alternatively, you could be a man about it and take on the challenge of looking after your offspring with the aid of our survival guide.

Prepare Yourself

While your partner is still at home, pay close attention to what she does. Learn the ropes and if you're very clever, start joining in. You might find washing the dishes or doing the vacuuming a chore, but bathtime, reading stories, and pillow fights (best to leave this until mom has actually gone) are all fun.

Learn Military Precision

No household can operate effectively without it. If it helps, make lists and a timetable. You need to remember what time school starts and what time it lets out. Choir rehearsals, music lessons, ballet classes, and soccer practice all happen on different days, at different times. Make sure you have directions to all the after-school activities and to places you don't normally go — like the doctor and dentist. You don't want to be running around like a lunatic, carrying a child that needs medical attention, when you've got no idea where you're going.

Cooking and Shopping

In the weeks prior to your partner's departure, start watching cooking programs and pay attention to how your partner prepares a meal. Ask her to provide you with a weekly shopping list so you don't overlook any essential items. You need to feed the children a balanced diet, although there should be room for treats (just keep them to a minimum, if you don't want the children bouncing off the walls).

If you don't normally feed your children certain foods, don't suddenly introduce them into their diet just because mom's away. It will add confusion — the younger the child, the more reassurance he or she will need while mom is not at home — plus it may cause upset tummies (spicy spareribs are not good for toddlers).

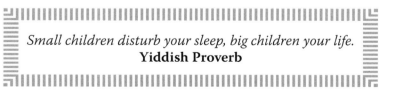

Small children disturb your sleep, big children your life.
Yiddish Proverb

Keep to the Children's Normal Routine

Children like routine: it makes them feel safe and secure. Don't let them stay up late with you, watching something unsuitable on TV. It will only lead to nightmares, tiredness, arguments, and tantrums — all of which you will have to deal with. If you have older children you are lucky, as chances are they will know exactly where to find everything, how the microwave works, and where mom keeps the cleaning supplies for when the cat throws up. Use this knowledge and ask for help, but don't abuse it and expect your older children to take over where mom left off.

If you do get help, always reward appropriately, perhaps by offering to let them have friends over.

Having coped admirably with the absence of your nearest and dearest, not only will you have reason to be proud of yourself, but your partner may start to see the "new" man in you. But be warned — this may lead to more domestic responsibilities for you in the long run.

If you are lucky, your partner will probably have put everything in place for you before she leaves. But, be prepared for the unexpected and keep smiling — even if that means gritting your teeth and going to bed early.

Little children, headache; big children, heartache.
Italian Proverb

Friends and Family

How to Keep Your Friends and Still Be with Your Family

As you are no doubt aware, having a child brings about the biggest change in your life, short of being hit by a train. You may have already noticed this if you have friends who have children. Remember that best friend you used to have? The one you could always count on to go out and have a good time, even if it was a Monday night? Well, if a baby could tame him, imagine what it will do to you! But don't worry, it is possible to strike a balance between being a father and an adult. Read on. . . .

Staying Friends

In order to deal with this change you need to cultivate relationships with your friends who already have children. Listen to the advice they offer on how to get your toddler to sleep at night or which is the best television program to let him or her watch — this will keep your child entertained for a while and give you some much-needed time to do a few household chores or put your feet up and catch forty winks!

Having friends with children also means that you can arrange to do things together, allowing you to have some adult company while the kids play. It can be a lot of fun when families get together and go out for the day, whether it's a barbecue or just a day in the park. Your friends might also be prepared to babysit your child at their house so you can enjoy an evening out with your partner. Just remember to reciprocate, or you'll find they won't offer again!

While raising your child is a lifetime responsibility, remember that when he or she has grown up and found his or her own way, you will have more freedom to do the things that you want to do so it's important to keep in touch with your friends. You won't be pulling your weight in the child rearing if you are out with your pals every night, but once in a while, it is definitely a good idea to get some time away from the family.

Relative Problems

Once you have a child, you'll find that your entire family will want to come and visit. Great-aunt Flossie will suddenly decide

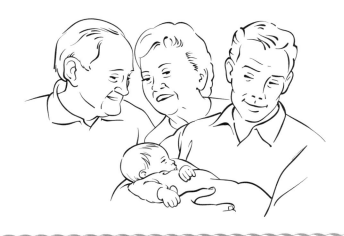

that, after twenty years, it's time she saw you again, time she met your partner, and time she came to stay for a week or two!

While it's perfectly acceptable for the newborn's grandparents and close aunts and uncles to want to see the baby, it's important to give yourselves time to adjust to your new roles as parents — especially just after coming home from the hospital or traveling home from your child's birth country.

Relatives will always have advice for you as a parent, whether you have asked for it or not! No matter how good a parent you are, at some point they will frown at the way you are dealing with a situation and say something like "My mother didn't do that!" or "It wasn't like that in my day!" Be diplomatic. Don't start arguing. Remember — the best thing about advice is that it is freely given but it doesn't *have* to be taken.

Love Thy Neighbor

Whether you get along with your neighbors or not will determine how you approach your relationship with them once you have a child. If they are friendly, you are more likely to try to keep the noise down and be embarrassed if your child is having a screaming tantrum at three in the morning. If you don't get along at all, then you probably won't be too worried about disturbing their sleep!

Joking aside, whether your neighbors are your best friends or not, making a real effort to stay on good terms with them will pay dividends in the long run. If you live in a neighborhood where noise travels easily, your neighbors will be more patient with the inevitable noise that a newborn baby can make if you have taken the time to butter them up a bit.

It is also far easier to ask a noisy neighbor to keep the racket down when you're trying to get the baby to sleep if you have made the effort to befriend them first. Try to be a considerate, good neighbor, and you will find that it often goes both ways.

Neighbors can also become great friends to you and your children. If they have kids themselves, then your child has playmates next door and you have friends with whom you can socialize.

If your neighbors are elderly, encourage your child to strike up a friendship with them. Your child will be fascinated by the stories they can recount of what life was like when they themselves were young. If they are able, they might enjoy joining you for a walk in the park or even doing a bit of babysitting every once in a while. If they are frail, they will be comforted by the thought that someone next door cares for them and is looking out for them.

Being good to your neighbors generally means that they will be good to you, too.

Human beings are the only creatures on Earth that allow their children to come back home.
Bill Cosby

How to Make a Bow and Arrow

If you really want to be a hero to your kids and impress them with your skills as an outdoorsman, go wrestle a bear or a crocodile. Alternatively, you could show them how to make a bow and arrow. Follow these instructions and, with a little practice, you'll be hitting a target at twenty paces in no time. Make sure you use an old dart board or something suitable as a target though. Try this out on the cat, no matter how much you hate the thing, and you'll go from hero to zero faster than a speeding arrow. A mound of soft dirt or sand in the yard will work well as a target. This will also help to preserve your arrows and make them easier to retrieve than chasing a wounded cat.

What You Need to Make Your Bow and Arrow

◆ A branch about 4 feet long and at least as thick as your thumb. Try to find or cut a straight length with little or no knots or offshoots. Yew is the traditional bow-making wood, but you can also use oak, elm, birch, or just about any other strong, healthy wood.

◆ As many straight, thin, 30-inch lengths of wood as you can find to be used as arrows.

◆ Some index cards to be used as the flights.

◆ Cord or twine

◆ Cotton thread

◆ A sharp knife

To Make the Bow

1 To make your bow bend and spring back you need to chamfer the ends. Mark the staff 1.5 feet from each end. Shave these end sections along the inside of the bow, tapering toward the tip. Always make sure to cut away from your body. You don't need to shave it too thin; you should slim the bow gradually until the tips are about half as thick as the middle. Next cut a thin groove in the unchamfered outside edge of the bow. The groove needs to be about 2 inches from the end. This is where you will tie your bowstring.

2 Tie the twine you are using as a bowstring to one end and bend the bow. Don't bend it too far — it needs to be able to bend further when you fire an arrow. Pull the bowstring taut and cut the required length.

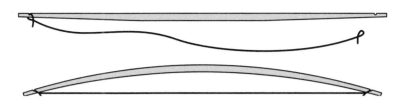

③ Make a loop in the open end of the string. Now slip this loop over the other end of the bow so that it sits in the notch. Always release the string when you are not using the bow so that the bow does not "set" in its bent shape and lose its power.

The Arrows

① The front of an arrow needs to be heavier than the back to prevent the arrow from tumbling through the air. Find the midpoint of the arrow by balancing it on your finger. Now you can tell which end (the shorter side) is heavier. Cut a slot in the lighter end and slide a piece of an index card cut in the shape of the feather below, so that it sticks out on either side of the slot. This will be your flight. Wrap some cotton thread ahead of the feather and behind it to squeeze the slot shut and clamp the feather in place.

② If you are feeling really macho, you can make an arrowhead by pounding a piece of flint into a thin blade or carving a sliver of bone. Arrowheads can be clamped in place using the same method you used for the flight. A very sharp arrowhead is, of course, extremely dangerous. It is safer and easier just to scorch the end of the arrow over a flame to harden it and then sharpen it with a knife. It is safer still to use a piece of modeling clay on the tip.

Now you are ready for target practice. You might want to wear a glove on your bow hand to protect you from the string because it can really sting if it catches your wrist and, unless you can turn your whimpering into an effective war whoop, you're going to look pretty stupid.

You can scale down the whole process to make bows for the kids. Now read the "Ten Best Threats" in this book to stop them from shooting you or one another. And remember, always supervise the target practice and, when finished, store the bows and arrows in a safe place where the children can't get them.

A babysitter is a teenager who gets two dollars an hour to eat five dollars' worth of your food.
Henny Youngman

Dads Then and Now

As a father, you were once indisputably head of your household. Nowadays, you're last in line for the bathroom. Fatherhood has changed significantly over the last century. Dads are expected to be more involved with their children, to play an active part in their upbringing, and, if you want to remain the family figurehead, you have to keep up with everything that today's independently minded kids are into.

Then
In 1900, fathers insisted that their children learned to read and write proper English.

Now
Fathers would like it if their children simply spoke some kind of recognizable English.

Then
In 1900, a father's horsepower meant his horses.

Now
It's the size of his SUV.

Then
In 1900, if a father put a roof over his family's head, he was a success.

Now

It takes a roof, pool, stable, and four-car
garage . . . and that's just the vacation home.

Then

In 1900, a father waited for the doctor to tell him
when the baby arrived.

Now

A father must wear doctor's scrubs,
know Lamaze breathing, and make sure
the digital video camera is fully charged.

Then

In 1900, fathers passed on clothing to their sons.

Now

Kids wouldn't be seen dead wearing your clothes!

Then
In 1900, fathers could count on teaching
their children the family business.

Now
Fathers pray their kids will come home from college
long enough to teach them how to use the computer.

Then
In 1900, a father smoked a pipe
or an after-dinner cigar.

Now
If he tries that, he'll be sent outside
with a lecture on lung cancer.

Then
In 1900, fathers shook their children gently
and whispered, "Wake up, it's time for school."

Now
Kids shake their fathers violently at 5.00 A.M. shouting:
"Wake up, it's time for football practice!"

Then
In 1900, a father came home from work to find his wife
and children at the dinner table.

Now
A father comes home to a note: *Joe's at soccer,*
Carol's at the gym, I'm at yoga, pizza in the fridge.

Then
In 1900, fathers and sons would have heart-to-heart
conversations while fishing in a stream.

Now
Fathers pluck the headphones
off their sons' ears and shout,
"WHEN YOU HAVE A MINUTE . . ."

Then
In 1900, if a father had breakfast in bed,
it was eggs, bacon, sausage, and toast with butter.

Now
Special K, semi-skimmed milk, dry toast,
and a lecture on cholesterol.

Then
In 1900, fathers said, "A man's home is his castle."

Now
Fathers say, "Welcome to the money pit."

Then
In 1900, a happy meal was when a father shared
funny stories around the table.

Now
A Happy Meal is
what a dad buys at McDonald's.

Then
In 1900, when fathers entered the room,
children rose to their feet.

Now
Kids glance up and grunt,
"Dad, you're blocking the TV."

Then
In 1900, fathers demanded to know
what prospects their daughter's suitors had.

Now
Fathers break the ice by saying,
"So . . . how long have you had your nose piercing?"

Then
In 1900, fathers were never truly appreciated.

Now
In the twenty-first century,
fathers are never truly appreciated.

*Heredity is what sets the parents of a teenager
wondering about each other.*
Laurence J. Peter

How Father's Day Came to Be

Let's face it, nobody makes as big a deal about Father's Day as Mother's Day. Dads have a long way to go before they catch up on the sort of fuss that is made over moms on Mother's Day. There's no point in complaining about it, though, because that just makes you look ungrateful for the homemade card and the new air freshener for your car. We should remember, too, that Father's Day was invented by a woman, and be suitably thankful.

Sonora Dodd came up with the idea for Father's Day while listening to a Mother's Day sermon in 1909. Sonora wanted a day to honor her father, William Smart, who was widowed when his wife died giving birth to their sixth child. Mr. Smart was left to raise the newborn and his five other children by himself on a farm in eastern Washington state.

The First Father's Day

When Sonora grew up, she realized the selflessness her father had shown in raising his children as a single parent. Sonora's father was born in June, so she chose to hold the first Father's Day celebration in Spokane, Washington, on June 19, 1910.

President Calvin Coolidge backed the idea in 1924, but it wasn't until 1966 that Lyndon Johnson signed a presidential proclamation declaring the third Sunday of June to be Father's Day. This was finally signed into law in 1972 by Richard Nixon.

The First Day of School

The first day of school can be both an exciting *and* stressful occasion for children and parents alike — exciting because it's a milestone event, stressful because it means separation. Whether your child is starting day care, preschool or elementary school, there are many simple things you can do to help prepare them for this new adventure.

Help your child adjust to the feeling of not having you around by leaving them with a relative or friend for a few hours. It will give your child the reassurance of knowing that you haven't abandoned him or her and that you'll be back!

Social skills such as the ability to share, take turns, and participate in a group are excellent tools for your child to learn. This makes the child better prepared to deal with new people and situations. Children can start to learn these skills at baby groups or toddler sessions.

Is the new school a good fit for your child? Do *your* homework, go along to open house days, and, if possible, take your child. Speak to the teachers, ask questions, and try to see the school in action.

Is your child's physical development age-appropriate? Children of school age should be able to feed themselves, use the toilet, go up and down stairs, and dress themselves. If they are struggling, help them learn for themselves — don't do everything for them.

There are a number of things you can do to help prepare your child for that first-day adventure:

Be positive and reassure your child that school is a good place. Role-play some enjoyable school activities to which your child can look forward. Preparation is everything: Get all your child's school supplies ready before the big day.

Going to the Classroom

Many schools allow you to go into class on the first morning to help your child get settled. Don't be too concerned if your little one cries or refuses to leave your side; teachers are used to this happening. You must let the teacher take charge of your child when the teacher thinks the time is right so that he or she can build a trusting relationship. All children react differently to being left in the teacher's care, and some make more of a fuss for far longer than others. Be assured that the morning routine will quickly become familiar and that any associated tantrums will be short-lived.

Try to help your child find a friend! Hopefully your child will be starting school with a familiar face from any preschool groups you've attended.

After a few days, you will wonder why you were so worried. You will barely merit a second glance from your child as he or she bounds into school with all his or her new friends!

Dad's Night In

Every so often, you have to let the lady of the house go out for an evening with her girlfriends. It is, after all, the only way you can properly justify your own nights out. This, of course, leaves you in charge of the kids. Try to remember that part — *you're* in charge, not them. The only way to survive is to plan an effective "hearts and minds" campaign well in advance. Figure out ways to keep them entertained that will also be fun for you. That's the key — make the whole evening fun and you will enjoy yourself, too.

One of the first hurdles you have to clear is feeding time. You can, of course, search through the many takeout menus stuck to the fridge door, but it's much more fun to make a pizza together and watch your favorite movie.

Easy-Bake Oven Pizza for One

Ingredients:
2¼ teaspoons milk • 2 tablespoons flour
⅛ teaspoon baking powder
dash of salt • 1 teaspoon margarine
1 tablespoon tomato sauce
1½ tablespoons shredded mozzarella cheese

1. Preheat the oven to 375° F.

2. Slowly adding milk to the mixture, stir together the flour,

baking powder, salt, and margarine until the dough looks like medium-size crumbs.

③ Shape the dough into a ball. (Add more flour if it's too sticky.) Put the ball into a greased pan.

④ Use your fingers to pat the dough evenly over the bottom of the pan, then up the sides.

⑤ Pour the tomato sauce evenly over the dough, and then sprinkle with cheese.

⑥ Add toppings of choice.

⑦ Bake for twenty minutes or until golden.

⑧ Slice and enjoy!

Movie Time

You don't have to wait until it's mom's night out to have a family movie night. Movies are an escape, so you need the right atmosphere — a darkened room, plenty of comfy seating, and snacks are a must. If you need to schedule an intermission for bathroom or refreshment breaks, do so to stop unnecessary interruptions. If there are disagreements about what to watch, write the movie titles on pieces of paper, fold them up, and pick one from a hat. If there are still moans and groans, you decide. Remember you *are* supposed to be in charge.

*If you've never been hated by
your child, you've never been a parent.*
Bette Davis

Ten Ways to Get Some Peace and Quiet

1. Get your parents/family to take the children out. On an outing, that is, not like a sniper would.

2. Buy all your kids headphones for the TV/DVD/CD players and make sure they will work for their computer games, too.

3. Lock yourself in the closet in your bedroom.

4. Convert your basement into a mini–theme park.

5. Trick out your shed with a PlayStation/TV and/or stereo just for you — remember to buy a padlock.

6. Treat your partner each time it's her birthday (or yours) to a night away at a hotel and get your relatives to look after the children. Remember to go home again.

7. Build an outhouse in the backyard where you can disappear with the Sunday papers.

8. Keep up your hobbies — your partner won't deny you time to do these and it will give you the perfect excuse for time on your own. If your favorite hobby is climbing Mount Everest, all the better.

9. Buy a one-man tent, put it up in the backyard, and pretend you are trekking across Antarctica. Remember to do this

only in wintertime, so that there is little chance the rest of the family will want to come, too.

10. Buy a second home that needs some fixing up, and go there on the weekends to do some work on it. Remember to take a newspaper, books, and a radio to listen to the game. Forget to take your cell phone.

As a parent you try to maintain a certain amount of control and so you have this tug-of-war. . . . You have to learn when to let go. And that's not easy.
Aretha Franklin

Things You'll Never Hear a Dad Say

◆ "Well, how about that? I'm lost! Looks like we'll have to stop and ask for directions."

◆ "Here are the keys to my new car — GO CRAZY!"

◆ "Your mother and I are going away for the weekend. Invite some friends over and have a party!"

◆ "I don't know what's wrong with your car. Just have it towed to a mechanic and pay whatever he asks."

◆ "No son of mine is going to live under this roof without a tattoo. Now quit whining and let's go get you one!"

◆ "What do you want a job for? I make plenty of money for you to spend."

◆ "I don't think age matters in a relationship — after all, he's only fifteen years older than you."

◆ "Here's my PIN number and debit card."

◆ "Of course you can go to an all-night party — call me at four A.M. and I'll pick you up."

◆ "Father's Day? Don't worry about that — it's no big deal."

How to Teach Your Child to Ride a Bike

Remember learning to ride your first bike without training wheels? Remember how scared you were? Remember how your dad giggled? Now it's your turn.

Learning to ride a two-wheeler is an important milestone in any child's life and as a dad you won't want to miss it. It's not all fun, though. You'll be the one jogging alongside the bike for miles with your back bent at a hideously unnatural and painful angle so that you can reach down to steady the bike by gripping the back of the seat while every turn of the pedals scrapes another layer of skin off of your shin. Why on earth would you want to miss that?

Preparation

◆ Make sure the bike is the right size for your child.

◆ Install training wheels if not already fitted.

◆ Buy the proper size helmet and make sure your child wears it every time he or she rides.

◆ Consider knee and elbow pads as well.

◆ Be sure the clothing your child wears is protective and not so loose that it will get caught up in the bike.

◆ Explain the importance of biking in safe locations and of wearing protective clothing.

◆ Discuss what to do if your child falls, and explain that this is part of the learning process.

◆ Find a safe place to learn. A field with short, hard-packed grass or a path surrounded by grass is ideal. There should be plenty of open space, flat ground, and no traffic.

Biking

◆ Get your child onto the bike and pedaling, while you walk alongside him or her.

◆ Ask your child to think about balancing on the wheels of the bike only. Explain that eventually you will take off the training wheels.

◆ Let your child ride the bike as often as possible with the training wheels. Be sure he or she learns how to stop effectively.

Training Wheels Off

◆ Only remove the training wheels when your child is totally comfortable riding the bike.

◆ Take hold of bike and child — the seat of the bike and the back of the child's sweatshirt, or one handlebar and the sweatshirt.

◆ Push and run along with the child, instructing him or her to keep pedaling and to look straight ahead.

◆ Take your hand off the seat when you feel the child balancing on his or her own.

◆ Encourage your child as you take your hand from his or her sweatshirt.

◆ Repeat the previous three steps until the child is able to start pedaling without you.

There may be a few crashes and tumbles, but children are remarkably resilient and, with a few words of comfort and a hug, your youngster will get back on the bike. All children want to be able to ride like the older kids. They may need a couple of sessions but, once your child has mastered the art of pedaling and balancing, he or she will progress very quickly.

You have a right to feel proud, but there's also a hint of sadness when you see your child cycling off on his or her own. It's one more little thing for which they no longer need you!

Getting the Kids to Bed on Time

When there's something you want to watch on TV, or you have some friends over for dinner, getting the kids to bed can be a nightmare. They don't like to be left out. Putting them to bed, and persuading them to stay there, can involve using all your best bribes and threats. The best way to tackle it is to make sure that they are good and ready for bed.

Exercise

School may be a mental challenge, but your kids certainly won't be physically exhausted. Make sure they have plenty of fresh air and exercise. If it's possible, walk to and from school rather than taking the car. Walk the dog, play in the park, go swimming, or sign them up for after-school sports. If children don't expend enough energy during the day, they are likely to have trouble falling asleep at night.

Homework

Don't leave homework until late in the evening. If there are a number of tasks to be completed, put these in order of importance and make sure that everything that is needed is on hand before starting. Check that there are no distractions, and have a quiet study area.

Prepare for the Next Day

Before bedtime, have all items ready for the next day. A clear mind will aid in getting good sleep. Keep a "to-do" list as a reminder of what things are needed for different classes. Homework assignments, athletic equipment, or musical instruments can be ticked off the list when laid out and ready.

Mealtime

Try to have a family meal together at a reasonable time. Use the time to chat about your day and theirs. Avoid stimulants such as soda, chocolate, or candy.

Wind Down

Once the work and chores of the day are completed, have some fun — it can't be all work and no play. Let your kids have some free time to wind down and do what they want to do. After all, they are children. . . .

Routine

The number-one way to eliminate bedtime battles is to establish a ritual and stick with it no matter what. Even though your kids may object at first, they will get used to it.

Relaxation

A nightly warm bath slows the heart rate, relaxes muscles, and aids a restful night's sleep. Bath time can be fun, too, but don't let the bubble fights or naval battles drag on too long.

Quiet Time

Nearly there! Choose a favorite storybook, get your kids tucked in bed, and read away. If they are old enough to read themselves, involve them by taking turns reading. You might also give them time to read by themselves for ten minutes before lights out.

Good night and sweet dreams. Now what was it you wanted to watch on TV?

Tips for a Stress-Free Morning

With time at a premium, a line for the bathroom, and grumpy family members everywhere, dads need to have a strategy for surviving early-morning madness.

Don't always blame the children for the way you feel in the morning. If you feel grumpy and stressed, this will rub off on the children and make them feel resentful and grumpy, too.

A non-negotiable routine is a requirement, not an option. It must be established with clear consequences. For instance, if your child doesn't get up the first time they are asked, their bedtime will be fifteen minutes earlier that night.

Morning Essentials

Although these require planning, they often save time in the long run and avoid battles and disagreements.

◆ Have a running order for the bathroom and make it clear that if you snooze, you lose!

◆ Have all uniforms/clothes laid out and ready. Doing this the night before means one less thing to do in the morning.

◆ At the start of autumn, don't wait until the first frost to find that missing glove in the closet. Plan ahead and have clothing, shoes, hats, and scarves ready. Do this for each new season.

◆ Make sure sports equipment and special items for class are ready. The last thing you need is to be asked for ingredients for a cake at seven A.M.

◆ Check that schoolbags are packed with any necessary homework. Nothing's worse than remembering the homework is on the kitchen table when you're halfway to school.

◆ Breakfast is important. Many experts argue that it is the most important meal of the day, so your kids need a nutritious start. Decide on breakfast choices and even set the table the night before.

◆ Why not carve out ten or fifteen minutes to yourself to have a relaxing shower and cup of coffee or a little exercise routine before the children wake?

◆ If your children do not wake by themselves, try playing some soft music or an audio story ten minutes before they need to get up.

Remember to talk, too. Chat about the fun things you can do together after school or on the weekend. You need to keep things positive and happy for a good start to the day. And above all, keep smiling!

Pocket Money —
What it Will Cost You!

Just accept it — you and your partner are the family bankers. You don't get to charge interest or call in loans; your banking system is more of a one-way cash flow with none of it trickling in your direction. As your children grow older, you'll find you have more to do and less time to do it. You will have to make time for running them around to their friends' houses, taking them to after-school activities like football, ballet, or music lessons, and helping them with their (more-complicated-by-the-year) homework.

To give yourself time to do these things, it's vital that you get the kids "trained" at an early age to help around the house, and the best way to do that is bribery! You can't call it anything

else, because if it weren't for the monetary reward the odds are that they simply wouldn't do it.

You can start them off with little jobs like tidying up the toys in their room and putting their dirty clothes in the hamper. Once they get a little bit older, they can help their younger siblings get dressed and ready for school. When they can be trusted not to break things, they can progress to putting away the dishes and making their own sandwiches, and by the time they approach their teenage years, they'll be ready to cut the grass or wash the car.

Older and Wiser

Of course, the older they get and the more complex the household chores they tackle, the greater the financial reward they will expect. Whereas you were paying your eight-year-old a dollar or two a week to do several sinks full of dishes, your twelve-year-old will realize that taking your car to the car wash costs you ten dollars, so they will expect a fee closer to this for performing the task in the driveway.

Whatever the financial damage to your wallet, it's worth getting the children to help out because it allows you some time to put your feet up or to do something that you enjoy — providing that they've left you with some pocket money, too!

Telling a teenager the facts of life
is like giving a fish a bath.
Arnold H. Glasow

How to Make a Kite

Technical Terms

A simple kite is made from these basic components:

1. The spine — the vertical stick you build your kite around.

2. The spars — the support sticks, placed crossways or at a slant over the spine.

3. The frame — joining spine and spars, this forms the shape of the kite and makes a support for the cover.

4. The sail — the paper, plastic, or cloth that covers the frame.

5. The bridle — one or more strings attached to the spine or spars, which helps control the kite in the air.

6. The flying line — the string running from the bridle, which you hold to fly the kite.

7. The tail — a long strip of paper or plastic or ribbon that helps balance the kite in flight. Not all kites need tails.

What You Need to Make a Diamond-Shaped Kite

◆ Thin garden twine

◆ Scotch tape or glue

◆ 1 sheet of strong paper (40 inches x 40 inches)

◆ 2 strong, straight wooden sticks of bamboo or wooden dowelling 35 inches and 39 inches

◆ Markers, paint, or crayons to decorate your kite

◆ Scissors

1. Make a cross with the two sticks, the shorter stick (spar) placed horizontally across the longer stick (spine). Center the spar so that each of its sides is equal in length.

2. Tie the two sticks together with string, making sure that they are at right angles to each other. A dab of glue can be used to help secure them in place.

3. Cut a notch at each end of the spine and spar deep enough to hold the type of string you are using. Then, cut a piece of string long enough to stretch all around the kite frame. Make a small loop in the string and lay this through the top notch, then tie the string around the spine below the notch. Wrapping the string around the top of the spine a couple of times will help to fasten it tightly.

4. Stretch the string down through the notch at one end of the spar. Then stretch it on down to the bottom of the

spine, fastening it as you did at the top, laying another small loop through the bottom notch.

⑤ Next stretch the string up through the notch at the other end of the spar and back to the top of the spine where you need to tie it off tightly, wrapping it around the spine again a couple of times, and cut off any string you don't need. This string frame must be taut, but not tight enough to warp the sticks.

⑥ Lay the sail material flat and place the stick frame face down on top. Cut around it, leaving about an inch for a margin. Fold these edges over the string frame and tape or glue them down so that the material is tight.

⑦ Cut a piece of string about 47 inches long, and tie one end to the loop at the top of the spine and the other end to the loop at the bottom. Tie another small loop in the string just above the intersection of the two crosspieces. This will be the kite's bridle, the string to which the flying line is attached.

8. Make a tail by tying a small ribbon roughly every 4 inches along the length of string. Attach the tail to the loop at the bottom of the kite.

9. Decorate!

Tips

◆ Cut *away* from you! It is safer and gives you more control over the scissors or knife.

◆ Improve stability by tying a bow onto your kite's tail.

◆ Hold your kite up by the string when you are finished to see if it is balanced. You can balance it by gluing more paper on the lighter side.

Safety

◆ Never fly kites near airfields, overhead power lines, roads, or railways.

◆ Do not fly kites in thunderstorms.

◆ Avoid flying kites over the heads of people or animals.

◆ Wear protective gloves, especially for larger kites in strong winds.

◆ Avoid other kites.

◆ Wear good sunglasses if you are looking up a lot on a sunny day.

In the Garden with Dad

If you enjoy gardening, the last thing you need is a "little helper" trampling your flower beds and ripping out seedlings instead of weeds. To help avoid having to watch your garden sanctuary fall victim to the good intentions of your children, here are some creative diversions to help keep them occupied while you work on your own little piece of paradise.

Bug Box

Children are fascinated by all of the things that you would rather not see in your garden. Spiders and flies, ladybugs and aphids, slugs and snails, pill bug, and ants — kids just love them. Bug hunting is one way of keeping them occupied while you garden.

Buy or make a bug box, which is usually a plastic cube with a magnifier built into the lid. Anything placed inside the box is magnified through the lid. The small size allows it to be easily carried in your pocket and is just the ticket for viewing bugs, rocks, or plant material.

Start by looking in your own garden: Some creatures live behind bushes or among flowers and grass, while others crawl beneath rocks, burrow underground, or swim in ponds. You can check what should be around at certain times of the year by looking things up on the Internet or visiting your local library.

You can also organize a garden quiz:

◆ Identify the most common insects in your region.

◆ Identify the characteristics of each insect.

◆ Describe the process of meta-morphosis of a caterpillar to a butterfly.

◆ Identify the various roles of bees such as queen, workers, etc. in making honey.

◆ Identify the parts of an ant's anatomy and the roles within an ant colony.

Ground Force

There are few things children enjoy more than planting seeds, watching them grow, and harvesting what they have grown. And this helps them learn that potatoes and carrots come from the earth — not the supermarket.

Make it fun for them by planting seeds that mature quickly and are large enough for a child to handle easily. Sunflowers are perfect if you have room in your garden.

Vegetables are also a good choice for young children. They germinate quickly and can be eaten when mature. Growing vegetables may even motivate your children to eat them every once in a while.

To add some color to the vegetable garden, you might want to add some flowers such as marigolds or sweet peas. Be sure any flowers you plant are nontoxic.

If your child appears to be developing green fingers, when it comes to their birthday or Christmas, why not buy them kid-size garden tools such as a rake, shovel, or spade — or maybe his or her very own wheelbarrow?

During the winter months, try keeping the children busy by planting pots with spring flower bulbs, which are also great Christmas gifts for relatives or teachers.

Most children enjoy Halloween and having a jack-o-lantern on the doorstep. Growing your own in the garden takes a fair amount of space, but can be a worthwhile project — especially once the kids get to carve and enjoy something they've grown.

During the summer months, collect flower petals and leaves for pressing. Either press between blotting paper inside a heavy book or purchase a small flower press. Your child can enjoy hours of fun creating handmade gifts such as cards, bookmarks, or pictures for family and friends.

If you don't have a garden, try using pots or containers on a windowsill. Herbs are a good choice to plant indoors for children because they grow fast and can then be tasted.

Feathered Friends

Another way of making the most of your garden is by encouraging birds to nest and feed. If you don't have a bird book on your bookshelf, visit your local library for more information.

Begin by identifying the birds and for a closer look use a pair of binoculars. Make lists of the different species that visit your garden and in a timeframe of, say, ten minutes count the number of different birds that appear.

Keep your garden birds fed by making a simple bird feeder. This is what you will need to do:

1 Modify a yogurt container

Carefully make a small hole in the bottom. Thread string through the hole and tie a knot on the inside. Leave enough string so that you can tie the cup to a tree or shrub.

2 Prepare some lard

Allow some lard to warm up to room temperature, but don't let it melt. Once it's warm, cut it up into small pieces and put it in a mixing bowl.

3 Add some tasty treats

Add birdseed, raisins, and grated cheese to the soft lard and mix together. Keep adding the dry mixture until the fat holds it all together.

4 Chill the bird cakes

Fill your yogurt container with the bird-cake mixture and put it in the fridge for an hour or so to set.

5 Add the finishing touch

Carefully cut away most of the sides of the yogurt container without disturbing the hardened bird cake inside. You should leave the base and part of the sides of the container. Then hang your bird cake from trees or shrubs.

Family Pets

Just because your kids decided they just had to have a pet when they saw a puppy in the park doesn't mean you should rush out and buy them one, no matter how much they pester you. Pets can teach children responsibility and provide love and companionship, but there are many questions to ask yourself — and them — before you add a pet to your family.

Are You Willing to Take on the Added Responsibility?

Before you ask whether your child is ready, you should start by asking if YOU are ready for a pet. The ultimate responsibility for a pet is in your hands. A pet is likely to make changes in your life. Some pets can be just as time-consuming as a newborn baby.

When Is the Right Time?

Just because the neighbor's dog had the most adorable puppies does not mean you should adopt one. Consider the decision carefully. It's probably not the right time to get a new pet if you have a child in the house who is under the age of two, you are planning to move, or a vacation is around the corner. Put at least a month's thought into the decision.

Is Your Child Ready?

With your supervision, children as young as three can help care for a pet.

◆ They can play gently with the pet.

◆ They can give the pet treats.

◆ They can fill food and water dishes.

◆ They can brush and groom cats and dogs.

◆ They can give love, attention, and respect.

Even though young children can be involved in pet care, they aren't ready to take over fully until their teenage years. Adults need to oversee the job to make sure that the child does what is necessary to take care of the animal properly. Animals should not suffer neglect because children are only beginning to learn responsibility.

A Few Things to Teach Your Child About Animals

◆ Never touch an animal's food.

◆ Wash hands after touching an animal.

◆ Let an adult clean up animal waste.

◆ Avoid teasing or provoking an animal.

◆ Pay attention to ways an animal tells you it doesn't like what you are doing. Help your child "listen" to the animal.

Keeping pets is an educational and fun way to introduce kids to responsibilities. The key to a successful pairing lies in choosing the appropriate pet for your child's abilities, age, and interests, as well as what you're willing to tolerate in the house.

Wait until your child expresses an interest in getting a pet. If you bring one home for him or her before he or she mentions it, there's a very good chance that he or she will be disinterested, and you've just given yourself a new pet to care for.

Discuss the animal in question with your child. If you're not willing to have certain animals around, make sure you suggest alternatives.

Research the different possibilities together with your child. Libraries have hundreds of animal-care books, or browse the pet section at a bookstore.

Read up on whichever pet you both decide on *before* you buy it. There may be aspects of its care and feeding that you weren't initially aware of, making it more or less suitable.

If possible, buy the necessary supplies such as a bed, cage, litter box, and toys a day or so before you get your pet.

Warnings

Your child may lose interest in whatever animal you choose, no matter how enthusiastic they are in the beginning. If you're not willing to become the animal's sole caretaker, you should not be considering bringing a pet into the household. If circumstances conspire to make it impossible for you to keep a pet you have bought, make arrangements well in advance with a friend who will adopt it.

If your goal in giving your children a pet is to teach them responsibility, make sure you are being responsible yourself. Finding a new home for an animal or taking it to a shelter when the kids lose interest only teaches them that responsibilities can be abandoned once you decide you're bored. If the whole family is not willing to make sure the new animal is cared for throughout its lifetime, get your child a plant or a virtual pet instead.

Low-Maintenance Pets

Taking your child's dog for a walk at night when it's freezing cold and raining is nobody's idea of fun. Neither is waking up thinking you're having a heart attack, with a strange tightness in your chest and a feeling of breathlessness, only to find the cat sitting on you.

If your offspring want a pet, but you don't think the novelty will take long to wear off, or you don't like animals yourself, here are a few suggestions for pets that require almost no maintenance.

Pet Rocks

Back in 1975, businessman Gary Dahl came up with this great idea and for a while it was the biggest fad. Here was a pet that required no care and gave its owner a few moments of pleasure. They were, however, easily lost if you left them out in the garden and didn't really return any of the affection lavished upon them. They were as good as a guard dog for protecting your home, though, because you could throw them at a burglar.

Stick Insects

They might not do much, but stick insects are a fascinating low-maintenance pet. There are more than 3,000 species, and they all feed exclusively on vegetation. They are relatively easy to handle, but you have to be careful with them; cages should be at the right temperature and humidity (as close to the wild as possible) and size; the insects need to be able to hang on to the vegetation to feed and live.

Ant Farms

You don't even need to find the ants yourself — ant farms are available through various retail outlets. They are compact and will sit in a corner of your abode, are simple to put together and when the inhabitants arrive, you can feed them your organic kitchen waste.

Goldfish

Fish are one of the easiest animals to keep as pets. They require little looking after, although they do require a proper tank that gives them enough oxygen (traditional goldfish bowls don't provide this). They should be fed every couple of days with specially prepared food, and their water should be changed every week or so. To keep their home fresh and clean, plants can be added to the aquarium tank and a filter is a good idea.

Tadpoles

You'll need a garden for this, and check that you don't harvest the spawn from a protected area as some frog populations are declining in the wild. Find some spawn, leave it in your own pond in the backyard and it will eventually hatch into tadpoles, which will turn into froglets. Frogs are great friends of the gardener, feeding on all types of unwanted insects and pests — and as wild creatures they don't require any care. Just provide them with some stones for shelter and some plant cover.

Tortoises

Though rapidly disappearing from their countries of origin, tortoises are still available and make good, easy pets — but you do need a fenced yard that has plenty of cover because they like to roam. They need regular water and food such as lettuce, tomatoes, dandelion leaves, and other fruits and vegetables. When autumn comes, place them in a wooden box with plenty of straw, and keep the box in a shed or garage where they will be protected from the cold. Your tortoise will hibernate until the spring because they are cold-blooded reptiles and cannot survive harsh cold spells.

Snakes

They may not be everybody's idea of a fun pet, but snakes are relatively easy to look after — they need warmth and a safe place to live like an aquarium-type tank. One thing to be aware of is that they like live food such as insects (grasshoppers) or mice.

Hamsters

One of the cutest pets are hamsters which are rodents like mice and guinea pigs. They don't require a huge amount of care, but they do need a nice spacious cage with some toys or exercise equipment. They also need to be watered and fed regularly. Buy nuts and seeds for them from the local pet store. The cage will need to be cleaned out twice a week. Regular handling usually makes hamsters tame and friendly.

Rabbits

Unlike rodents, rabbits are not for apartments and condos. Ideally, they need a hutch and a run in a yard for a good quality of life. They are easy to handle and one of the most popular small pets, but they are time-consuming. They need to be fed and watered daily and their cages regularly cleaned out — a job for poor old dad!

Small Birds

Budgies, canaries, and small parakeets make excellent house pets, but they do require some care. They need a spacious cage and/or access to fly around the room once a day. It's important to keep their beaks and claws short and, like all pets, they need to be fed, watered, and their cage regularly cleaned out. Budgies make especially good pets, and they are very rewarding. They are good mimics, friendly birds, and have a decent longevity if cared for properly. Ideally, small birds should be given the run of an aviary, but they are great escape artists and will make an attempt for freedom. Unfortunately, most don't fare well in the wild and won't survive for long.

> *Teenagers complain there's nothing to do, then stay out all night doing it.*
> **Bob Phillips**

Dad's Guide to Camping

Whether you're already a seasoned outdoorsman or not, camping is a great way to spend time with your children. It doesn't have to be expensive, plus it gets you out of the house and into the countryside for a few days!

If you want a true father-child experience, you can "rough it" in a small tent, carrying with you all the equipment you need. This might be fine for older children, but don't expect your two-year-old to lug a twenty-pound pack on a ten-mile hike to your campsite. For those dads who seriously want to get back to nature, there are campsites that allow you to pretend to be Grizzly Adams. Here you can trek through the countryside, pitch your tent in a forest clearing, and cook your food on an open fire, before scaring your child silly with ghost stories and then trying to get them to sleep. Knowing that there are some civilized facilities not too far away can be a comfort for both you and your child.

If the whole family is going or you'd like a bit more space when you're camping, then a bigger tent is a necessity. Unless you have a roomy SUV, you might need to consider investing in a trailer or roof rack to transport all the essentials needed to keep the family happy. This may include a fridge or ice chest, a portable DVD player (to keep the children quiet on rainy days), as well as games and books to keep the children entertained. Don't worry, most commercial sites have an electric hookup facility.

If you'd like a little more luxury, then consider a fifth wheel. Sure, you might have to trade in the car if it's a small hatchback, but if you already have a decent-size family car it should be okay for towing. Fifth wheels don't have to be expensive, but, as with everything else in life, you get what you pay for. Modern trailers will comfortably sleep two to six people, have hot and cold running water, a shower, and a toilet. They are perfect for inexpensive family vacations and are far more comfortable than a tent if the weather conspires against you.

There is nothing wrong with today's teenager that twenty years won't cure.
Anonymous

Perils and Pitfalls of Cell Phones

Cell phones are as much a part of our lives now as the television or the computer. However, as much as you may regret the fact that your boss, wife, mother, or lawyer can now reach you wherever they want, the cell phone has made itself indispensable. It comes as no surprise, then, that almost every child aspires to have his or her own cell phone. Acquiring a cell phone has become something of a rite of passage and the average age at which a child joins the cell-phone fraternity has now fallen to just eight. Before you equip your youngster with a phone, however, there are a number of questions that you really should address.

Cell-phone marketing companies can "spam" phones with advertising messages. Tell your child not to use their cell to enter competitions because that can involve a hefty charge.

Cell phones can become a "safety blanket" for children and be relied upon too much for help. Encourage your child to think first and not to call you for an easy answer.

Cell phones can be a distraction when used at inappropriate times. Make sure your child turns off the phone when at school, house of worship, the library, and other such places. The phone can also be a dangerous distraction when a child is crossing the street or just walking down the road because he or she is not fully aware of what is going on. Teach your children always to be aware of their surroundings.

Children may become vulnerable to others wishing to steal their phone. Stress the importance of security. They shouldn't go flashing a phone around to show off, and make sure you don't buy them an inappropriately expensive phone (they could start with one of your old ones).

Other people can run up bills if the phone is misplaced or stolen. Make sure your child has a pay-as-you-go phone with limited credit.

Children can quickly pick up bad "textspeak" habits. Keep an eye on their school assignments to ensure they are not using inappropriate abbreviations like "gr8" for "great."

Ten Classic Board Games

Computer games can be fun, but they've got nothing on the classic board games we grew up with. During those long winter nights and cold, wet weekends, turn off the TV and pull out some of the tried-and-trusted favorites like the ten listed below. They are a great way to pass the time and, unlike computer games, they also help to get your kids talking to you.

1. Chess
2. Clue©
3. Dominoes
4. Scrabble©
5. Monopoly©
6. Scattegories©
7. Risk©
8. Trivial Pursuit©
9. MouseTrap©
10. Pictionary©

How to Teach Your Child to Drive

The best tip of all is — hire a driving instructor! That way you are most likely to remain on speaking terms with your child. If you must teach your budding Dale Earnhardt yourself, the following tips may be helpful.

For some reason, teaching someone else to drive (unless you're professionally qualified) often means arguments and disputes. Learn to have patience. It will help keep the peace, show your child that you can see he or she is growing up and becoming responsible, and, most importantly, keep you out of the ER for having a heart attack or bursting a blood vessel.

First, check with your local Department of Motor Vehicles to see what permits are necessary in order to teach your child to drive. Once you have obtained these, the next thing to do is find a large, open space to begin the lessons. An empty parking lot or quiet residential street is ideal for this. Trying to teach a teenager hand, eye, and foot coordination is not easy, but if he or she is going to pass the test and stay safe on the road, it's important. They will be able to concentrate far better on practicing these basic skills if they don't have any other traffic to worry about.

Explain the gauges simply and clearly. Let your child start the engine and let him or her get a feel for the car. To a first-time driver, even the smallest compact car feels like a bus. If you are unlucky enough to be teaching in a car with a manual transmission, guide your child slowly into finding first gear and remain calm when they jerk their foot off the clutch and knock your head into the windshield before stalling. It's probably best if you keep your seatbelt on at all times.

Show No Fear

Try again. Eventually, your child will feel that bite, get the hang of it, and before you know it you'll be bumping along in first gear at 30 mph while your child grinds around for second. Do not let the fact that your clutch will never be the same worry you. And more importantly, do not let the driver see your white knuckles as you hold on to the door for dear life while your fingernails draw blood from your palms.

Praise is the key. Encourage all the things your child does right and keep the edge out of your voice when he or she makes a mistake. After a few (painful) sessions, he or she will have found fourth and fifth gears and if he or she is able to brake and come to a stop without giving you whiplash, it may be time to try the open road.

Teach your teenager the basics of the car — not just how to start, go, and stop, but also how to put oil in it. This involves taking out the dipstick and pointing out that the small hole it has come out of is not where you put the oil in. It's also wise to show your child where to pour the windshield-washer fluid.

This does not get splashed down the vents on the hood, but actually has its own container in the engine compartment. Show them how the gas tank cap goes on and off and teach them what to do at the gas station — including paying!

Get Help

After a few trips out in the car, your teenager will be starting to feel comfortable driving and it may then be time for you to take a backseat — no, not literally! Unless you are the very best of teachers, your child will now need a professional to coach them through their driving test. Your ideas about the rules of the road may be years out-of-date and, while you can provide your child with a basic understanding that will boost their confidence, lessons from a professional are what will bring them the coveted driver's license. For this professional help, you should look into private driver's education courses, or perhaps ones offered through your teen's school.

Be prepared to let the novice take the wheel when you go on short errands, as the more experience they have behind the wheel, the better.

Then, when your teenager has passed the driving test, you and your partner can look forward to being picked up and chauffeur-driven home after an evening out. The downside of that, of course, is that your car may be "borrowed" on a regular basis and the gas tank will never have quite as much fuel in it as you thought!

Choosing a Musical Instrument

You may have been tone-deaf all your life and have as much musical talent as your left shoe, but don't let that get in the way of encouraging your children to take an interest in music. Learning a musical instrument is a slow and, for anyone forced to listen, tortuous process, but it has all sorts of benefits for your child. While writing music is a hugely creative process, it also involves an orderly logic that has a very close relationship to mathematics. Learning to read music in order to play an instrument is wonderful mind-training for your child. Remind yourself of that when you are sitting with your fingers in your ears during violin or recorder practice at home.

The recorder is the obvious first choice. Although boys tend to find this a bit girlie, it's not. It's the foundation for learning more difficult instruments and will help them learn to read music. Although there are prodigies who can play an instrument without ever having learned to read music, they are few and far between. Unless your own father is David Bowie, and your child has inherited his musical genes, it's probably best to start your child off with learning the basics.

Unfortunately, the recorder is a screechy instrument in the wrong hands, and most young children are unable to understand the concept of blowing softly. This results in no actual notes, just shrill sheets of sound. Try to remain optimistic and hope they grow out of this instrument and move on to something more mellow.

Once your child has mastered the recorder (if you haven't thrown it out of the window first), he or she might show an interest in the clarinet. Hooray, we hear you shout. But don't get too comfy. This is a difficult instrument to learn. It's not an impossible instrument to learn, but it still takes time, effort, and (on your part) patience.

The piano is also a favorite. Although it can be expensive to buy and maintain, if you're very lucky, you can find a used one being sold or given away that is just in need of a tune. Otherwise, you could be looking at spending up to $3,000 on an electric piano. On the plus side, an electric piano comes with headphones that will save you from having to listen to hours of relentless scales.

Stringed instruments make a beautiful sound. Violins are angelic, while violas are mellow. Cellos resonate with clarity, and the double bass is downright funky. The trouble is that it takes a long time to learn how to make them sound their best and that will be stressful on your ears. The violin requires balancing a bowed stick with horsehair over four, fairly close together strings. These are made of fine steel (at least they don't use catgut anymore). This movement is quite a challenge. To make the job even more difficult, your child will need to use the fingers on the left hand to make the notes on the fingerboard. This is a feat unto itself because there's no markings to tell your child where to place his or her fingers — it's only through practice that they'll learn where the notes are. That's when your ears will really start to suffer. The better your child gets, the more he or she will be encouraged to wobble his or her fingers while playing a note. This is called vibrato. You will without a doubt come up with a few other names for it.

Brass instruments are no easier to master. Your child will need to learn breath control — that's where the recorder and blowing softly comes in — but you can't blow too softly or

else there won't be a note at all. Trumpets and cornets are popular, while trombones and French horns are more difficult.

Percussion is fun, but you need a big house, preferably with a soundproof garage. You will definitely need earplugs if your child is learning the drums!

Perhaps the guitar — classical, folk, or electric — is for your budding musician. These are affordable and easily cared for. There are many teachers around who charge competitive rates and you might find the next Eddie Van Halen, Eric Clapton, or Jimi Hendrix living in the same house as you!

Ten Best Threats

You can discuss things with kids; try to persuade them to do something; try to persuade them not to do something; try to reason with them; try to give them orders; and try all sorts of arguments to make them do what you want. They can, however, be the most stubborn and defiant creatures ever known to walk the face of the earth.

When all else fails, don't be afraid to use threats — and then don't be afraid to follow through on your threats. Here are ten of the best:

1. "If you _____ I'll tell your mother when she comes home."

2. "If you _____ you'll go to your room and stay there."

3. "If you _____ there'll be no more PlayStation for the rest of the week."

4. "If you _____ I'll take your bike back to the shop."

5. "If you _____ you'll be banned from football for the rest of the month."

6. "If you _____ you'll go to bed early."

7. "If you _____ you'll be grounded for a week."

8. "If you _____ I'll tell Uncle Dave that you don't deserve to go fishing."

9. "If you _____ you won't get any dessert, ever."

10. "If you _____ Santa Claus won't be coming this year."

How to Survive a Family Vacation

Gone are the days when you could pack a small bag of carry-on luggage and jet off for a couple of weeks in the sun without a care in the world. With a family to worry about, the most restful time of your year can turn out to be the most testing. The only way to make sure it all goes as smoothly as possible is to plan as you pack.

For kids, the excitement of preparing to go on vacation is a high that is tempered only by the extreme low of the boredom of hanging out at an airport or the endless car trip to your vacation destination. Therefore, when you pack your baggage, you need to bear in mind that you have to make the fun begin as soon as you leave home.

Be Prepared

Give each of the children a disposable camera. They'll take lots of pictures of walls, ceilings, and floors, but they'll enjoy the independence.

Pack the car the night before, and hide a surprise or two somewhere in the car that the kids can search for at rest stops.

Leave home at naptime or, better still, the early hours. The more your kids sleep in the car, the better for all.

Take a scrapbook, gluestick, pens, and scissors so they can make a collection of ticket stubs and postcards of where they have been and what they've done.

Don't forget the first-aid kit. You can buy these from most drugstores and, of course, take your cough and cold medicine, mosquito repellent, and sunscreen. If traveling overseas, check what vaccinations may be required.

Make sure your kids pack a backpack with a few toys, games, and books for the trip. Make sure these don't have lots of small pieces, because they will only get lost down the side of the car seat.

Don't do too much too soon! You may want your kids to experience the wonders of Egypt or a transatlantic trip to Europe, but take them at an age when they can appreciate what they are seeing and doing.

Kids are usually happiest doing the simple things. Don't make any trip or visit too complicated or try to cram in too much.

Day Trips

Avoid disagreements over which spots to visit by allowing each family member to look through the various guides and choose an attraction. Your kids may not be happy looking around the gardens of an historic house (unless you find one with a maze), but at least they know they will be able to choose the water park the next day. If choosing day trips causes constant arguments, set up a mystery tour to a destination of your choice. They can try to guess en route where they're going. When you get to the attraction, try letting the kids go into the gift shop before you set off to see the sights. Here are some more tips to help make your vacation as stress-free as possible:

◆ Don't choose destinations more than an hour's drive away. If it took you seven hours to get to your vacation accommodations, another trip of whining, diaper changes, and an endless supply of snacks really isn't worth it.

◆ Try to visit attractions midweek to avoid the crowds.

◆ When going out to restaurants, choose places with a reasonable level of background noise so you're not so conscious of the noise your own kids are making.

◆ Always carry a large supply of wipes!

◆ Give older teens some freedom to explore or be on their own. They'll appreciate the space and the opportunity for independence, as well as your confidence in their reliability and behavior.

◆ Always have a Plan B in case of bad weather or temper tantrums.

◆ Keep a cooler full of food and drinks, replenishing it daily with bottles of water, fruit, and snacks.

◆ When taking your kids on vacation, remember that they will be playing in an unfamiliar environment and that there may be potential hazards.

◆ Children don't always appreciate places and items of special interest, so avoid the headache of them being in a museum and clambering all over a priceless vintage car that doesn't mean a thing to them.

◆ Always carry an emergency bag in the trunk with a spare set of clothes and shoes for each child.

Two-Family Vacations

Going on vacation with another family has its advantages and disadvantages. You may end up never wanting to see the other family ever again, but if you're willing to take the risk, here are some pros and cons to consider:

◆ Having someone to babysit will enable you to have a few evenings out as a couple, and the same for your friends.

◆ Having other children around will help keep your own entertained.

◆ If possible, think about letting each child travel with each family, swapping at rest stops.

◆ Extra adults can lessen the responsibility.

◆ Once the kids are in bed, you can have a party!

◆ At least if your friends' children are badly behaved, it will make yours look like little angels.

◆ Differences in child discipline can cause friction. Other people's children never behave as you expect your own to.

◆ You don't know people until you live with them. Be prepared to discover your easygoing friends are actually really annoying!

◆ The children could decide they hate one another.

◆ Competitiveness over how to build the perfect sand castle or cook the perfect breakfast could lead to disaster.

Vacation Resorts

Instead of a traditional do-it-yourself vacation, why not consider a resort, where all your needs are taken care of at one site? Here are some of the benefits of an all-inclusive resort:

◆ If the resort is self-catering and specifically for families, it will probably provide everything you need, so there's no need to take everything but the kitchen sink with you — it's all already there.

◆ It gives you and the kids a chance to try all sorts of different activities, from archery or paintballing to horseback riding.

◆ They're excellent for short trips, because everything you need is on-site so you can use your time there efficiently.

◆ The price is all-inclusive, so you know exactly how much it will cost.

Taking Your Children Abroad

Many of the previous suggestions still apply, but take note of these more specific tips:

◆ Once your destination is decided, show the kids where they are going on a globe or in an atlas.

◆ Dehydration can contribute to jet lag, and airline cabins are notorious for their dry air. Make sure your child gets plenty of fluids during flight time.

◆ Consider traveling during off season to beat the crowds and high prices.

◆ Make sure you dress your kids for travel — layers are great, as are shoes that slip on and off with ease.

◆ Before you go, check the climate and pack appropriate clothing.

◆ Remember the travel insurance — probably compulsory in most vacation packages, however for independent travelers with children it is just as essential.

◆ Try learning some of the language and teach a few simple phrases to the kids.

On the Beach

However calm and tranquil a beach may look, there can be hidden dangers.

◆ Check the tide table before going swimming or ask the lifeguard for advice. Find out what warning signs and flags are displayed, know exactly what they mean, and ensure that young children are constantly supervised.

◆ Make sure young children know what to do and where to go if they lose sight of you.

At the Hotel

When you arrive at your hotel, ask the staff if there are any local hazards such as ponds on the hotel grounds or nearby cliffs.

◆ Check that the swimming pool is fenced off. Read any safety notices around the pool and obey them. Remember that babies under the age of four months should not be swimming at all, because they will not have had the correct vaccinations.

◆ Examine the stairwells around your hotel room, because they're unlikely to have stair gates.

◆ If you have a room with a balcony, check the height and width of any railings.

◆ Be aware of any sharp-edged furniture in your room.

◆ Make sure you know where the fire exits are located.

In Short

◆ Plan ahead.

◆ Perspective — put the vacation into perspective and stop trying to please everyone.

◆ Routine — regardless of the vacation, try to maintain some routine with children.

◆ Moderation — don't go overboard on vacation spending; budget and know your limit.

◆ Selection — pick and choose your vacation activities.

◆ Relax — vacations are meant to be enjoyed by everyone, including dads!

A successful man is one who makes more money than a wife can spend. A successful woman is one who can find such a man.
Lana Turner

Ten Best Bribes

1 "If you _____ I'll give you your allowance early."

2 "If you _____ I won't tell your mother."

3 "If you _____ I'll buy you a PS3."

4 "If you _____ I'll take you bowling on Saturday."

5 "If you _____ I'll take you to McDonald's."

6 "If you _____ I'll buy you some candy."

7 "If you _____ I'll get you a new bike."

8 "If you _____ you can stay up late tonight."

9 "If you _____ I'll let you go to the party/concert."

10 "If you _____ you can invite your friends over on Friday and I'll order pizza."

And my parents finally realize that I'm kidnapped and they snap into action immediately: They rent out my room.
Woody Allen

Are We There Yet?

Games for Long Car Rides

Once you have reached the point where you can't bear to hear the kids desperately trying to make up yet another verse to "The Wheels on the Bus" (*The one-legged giraffe with a sore throat on the bus goes . . .* is probably the limit), you can try a few other games.

Many of the games you can play in the car are probably games you played as a kid, but have forgotten all about. Keep in mind these games are also great for when you are in an airport or waiting for a table at a restaurant.

Here are ten great games for the car:

① Twenty Questions

The game of Twenty Questions is a true classic that can be played by children of all ages. There are many variations of the game.

One person thinks of something that falls under the category of person, place, or thing, and then tells the other players which category. The players then take turns asking questions that can be answered with a YES or NO. For instance, if the category is animal, a player might ask "Can it fly?" or "Does it have four legs?" And after twenty questions are asked, if the players have not already guessed the answer, each player gets a last chance to make a guess. Afterward, a new player tries to stump the group.

② Geography

Geography is not for younger children. This game is best for children aged eight and up. Not only do they enjoy the game, they know enough locations to be able to play the game well. Although the finer points may vary from place to place, this is how the basic game is played.

Someone starts by naming a country such as Japan. The next person must name a country whose name begins with the last letter of the previously named country. In this case, Japan ends in N, so a country that begins with N must be named, such as Nigeria. Then, since Nigeria ends in an A, the next person's country must start with an A. And so on, until someone gets stumped — he or she then drops out and the game continues until just one of you is left as the winner.

③ What's My Name?

A simple, yet fun game and perfect for children of all ages. Think of a name. Then tell the group whether it is a boy's name or a girl's name, and also tell them the first letter of the name. The group then tries to guess the name by calling out all the names they can think of that start with the appropriate letter. That's it. Simple, but fun!

④ Alphabet Memory Game

Good for children of all ages and an excellent way to help reinforce a preschooler's ABCs, yet fun for the elementary school age child, too!

The first person starts with the letter A and says "A is for —" filling in the blank with any word beginning with the letter A, such as APPLE, ARTICHOKE, or AIRPLANE. Let's use APPLE. The second person then does the letter B, but must also remember what A was! So, let's say the second person decides to use the word BOOK for B, the second person would say, "A is for APPLE and B is for BOOK."

You continue through the alphabet. By the time you get up to the letter Z, the player will have to recite each and every letter with its corresponding item. The game takes a while and kids love it, particularly if you throw in some silly words or phrases like S is for SMELLY TOES.

⑤ I Spy

The object of the game is to announce something that you spy (see) and have someone guess the correct answer.

It should be something you can see constantly, like the sky, or Dad's glasses, or the truck in front of you — not something that you pass quickly on the road.

To start the game, you say aloud, "I spy with my little eye something beginning with the letter M."

Have people ask you yes or no questions, one at a time, such as: "Is it Mommy?" or "Is it Dad's mustache?"

Whoever guesses the correct answer gets the next turn to spy.

You can simplify this to "I spy the color blue," for younger travelers, inspiring questions such as "Is it the sky?" or "Is it my sweatshirt?"

6 All About You

This is a good game to play when the sun goes down and you can't see much out of your car window.

Ask thoughtful questions of everyone in the car. Then take the time to listen to the answers and then discuss them.

It's a great way to learn more about the people you are traveling with!

Here are some questions you can ask to get started.

"If you could have lunch with any three people in the world, alive or not, who would they be and why?"

"If you won a million dollars in the lottery, what would you do with it?"

7 Guess the Number

Let your child think of a number in a stated range of numbers. You then try to guess the number by asking questions. Here's an idea of how it might go:

Your child: "I'm thinking of a number between 1 and 100."
You ask: "Is it more than 50?"
Your child: "No."
You: "Is it an even number?"
Child: "No."
You: "Can you divide this number into three equal parts?"
And so forth.

After you have guessed the number, let your child guess a number that you are thinking of by asking similar questions.

One benefit of this game is that by asking questions

about numbers, it helps your child to develop an understanding of some concepts, characteristics, and meanings of numbers. If he or she finds it difficult at first, this is an opportunity to explain and help him or her understand.

⑧ Red Car, Yellow Car, Blue Car . . .
Ask the children to choose a color or model of car of their choice. Set a time limit of ten or fifteen minutes, during which they have to mark down how many cars they see of their chosen color or model.

⑨ Who Am I?

Think of someone famous and give the other players a clue. For example, Elvis Presley could be hinted at by the description *singer* or the initials EP. The others take turns to guess who you are. Once the famous person has been guessed, the winner chooses the next celebrity.

⑩ What's My Job?

You will need to think of a profession, say a dentist, farmer, or train conductor, and give the players ten chances to guess your job by taking turns asking questions. You can act out the job as a clue, as long as you're not driving! The winner has the next turn at choosing a profession.

The young always have the same problem; how to rebel and conform at the same time. They have now solved this by defying their parents and copying one another.
Quentin Crisp

Ten Things Fathers Wish They'd Known

1. I wish I'd known what to expect. Maybe then I'd have all the right answers at just the right moments!

2. I wish I'd known that I should have written down all the hilarious things they said.

3. I wish I'd learned how to balance the art of listening and the desire to solve. Don't tell the children exactly the "right" answer before they've finished telling their problem.

4. I wish I'd treasured the special moments of laughing, wrestling, and telling silly stories.

5. I wish I'd known it takes about thirty-five minutes to clean Play-Doh off the floor, about forty-five minutes to get crayon marks off the wall, and about a week to remove any mark if combined with paint.

6. I wish I'd known what to do when the disposable diapers ran out in the middle of a park on a beautiful summer day.

7. I wish I'd known that a smile *always* helps.

8. I wish I'd known how to stay awake at Monday-night Scout meetings and Saturday-morning soccer practice.

9 I wish I'd known that children might listen to words but pay more attention to actions.

10 I wish I had realized that fatherhood is not something that can be acted, rehearsed, or imagined, but must be experienced every moment of each and every day.

Mother Nature is providential. She gives us twelve years to develop a love for our children before turning them into teenagers.
William Galvin, politician

Famous Fathers

It's always good to be able to remind your kids of how important fathers are, especially just before Father's Day. You may already be incredibly successful or famous, a respected businessman or captain of industry, a champion athlete or major figure in the arts — but to your kids you're just Dad.

To your child, of course, you are the most important dad to ever have walked the face of the planet, but if he or she occasionally doubts how vital fathers have been throughout history, here are a few examples to floor them with.

Father of Modern Computing — Alan Turing

At the time of his death in 1954, Alan Turing had already played a major role in the development of the intelligent computer. Headstrong, eccentric, and prone to solitary pursuits, Turing distinguished himself as a brilliant mathematician at King's College Cambridge, and later, at Princeton began work on proofs that established the foundation of the computer.

Father of Modern Science — Albert Einstein

German-born Albert Einstein was still in his twenties when he discovered new factors in the relation between water and energy. When he was twenty-six years old, he came up with his theory of relativity and light. After some time, he wrote a book called *The Year Book of Physics*. He completed his famous formulation E=mc^2 after he had a physical and nervous break-down and was sick for weeks. He published another book that established the theory for and potential effects of the splitting of the atom. The information from the books gave people the idea of the atom bomb, although Einstein never wanted his work to be used in that way.

Father of Freedom — Nelson Mandela

Nelson Mandela grew up in South Africa under the apartheid system of government that discriminated against nonwhite citizens. Starting out as a leader of an underground political movement called the African National Congress (ANC), Mandela played a part in many dramatic demonstrations against the white-ruled government. His career in the ANC was cut short in 1964 when he was sentenced to life in prison. But even then, Mandela continued to be a beacon of hope for his people who carried on the struggle in his absence. In 1990, after twenty-seven years of imprisonment, Mandela was freed. His release marked the beginning of the end of apartheid.

Father of Modern Biology — Charles Darwin

Charles Darwin did not dream up the idea of evolution, he was merely the first to put forward an explanation of how evolution works. Darwin developed the theory of natural selection. This is the idea that the environment in which an organism lives helps to determine which organisms survive and reproduce, and which do not. In 1859, Darwin published *On the Origin of Species*, a book that sold out the first day it was in print. It was also an immediate source of great controversy.

Father of Comedy — Charlie Chaplin

Charlie Chaplin was a comedic English actor, considered to be one of the finest mimes and clowns ever caught on film. Chaplin began in the silent-film era and acted in, directed, wrote, produced, and eventually even scored his own films. His working life in entertainment spanned more than seventy years, from the British Victorian stage and music hall in England as a child performer until his death at the age of eighty-eight. He led one of the most remarkable and colorful lives of the twentieth century, from a Dickensian London childhood to the pinnacle of world fame in the film industry.

Father of Rock 'n' Roll — Elvis Presley

Elvis Aaron Presley was a singer and actor regarded by many as one of the greatest entertainers of the twentieth century. He was the most commercially successful singer of rock 'n' roll after bursting onto the scene in 1954, but he also had success with ballads, country, gospel, blues, pop, folk, and even semi-operatic and jazz standards. In a musical career of more than two decades, Presley set many records for concert attendance, television ratings, and sales of recordings, becoming one of the bestselling artists in music history.

Father of Children's Books — A.A. Milne

Alan Alexander (also known as A.A.) Milne, was a British author and playwright. He is most famous for his Pooh books about a boy named Christopher Robin, based on his son, and various characters inspired by his son's stuffed animals, most notably the bear named Winnie-the-Pooh. (A Canadian black bear named Winnie, after Winnipeg, which was the military mascot of the Royal Winnipeg Rifles, a Canadian infantry regiment in World War I, was left to the London Zoo after the war and is presumed to be the source of the name.) E.H. Shepard illustrated the original Pooh books, using his own son's teddy bear, Growler, as the model. Christopher Robin

Milne's original toys are now in the New York Public Library collection.

Father of Puppeteers — Jim Henson

James Maury Henson was the best-known puppeteer in modern American television history as well as a film director and television producer. He was the creator of the Muppets (the name a cross between marionette and puppet) and the leading force behind their long creative run. Henson brought his engaging cast of characters, innovative ideas, and sense of timing and humor to millions. He is also widely acknowledged for the ongoing vision of faith, friendship, magic, and love that infused his work. *The Muppet Show* and *Sesame Street* television shows thrilled millions of children, including his own, who now carry on his legacy.

Father of Soccer — Pelé

"I was born for soccer, just as Beethoven was born for music." These are the words of Edson Arantes do Nascimento, the Brazilian genius known throughout the soccer world as Pelé, who burst onto the scene as a teenager in the late 1950s. A veteran of four World Cups, scorer of 1,283 first-class goals (twelve of them in World Cup final tournaments), and a member of those magical Brazilian squads that won soccer's greatest prize in 1958, 1962, and 1970, Pelé remains the undisputed King of Soccer. He ended his career in the United States where his presence gave the game a much-needed boost.

Father of Explorers — Christopher Columbus

Columbus's voyages of discovery across the Atlantic launched the European colonization of the Americas. While history places great significance on his first voyage of 1492, he did not actually reach the mainland of North America until his third voyage in 1498. Likewise, he was not the earliest European explorer to reach the Americas, as there are accounts of European transatlantic contact prior to 1492. Nevertheless, Columbus's voyage came at a critical time of growing national imperialism and economic competition between developing nation states seeking wealth from the establishment of trade routes and colonies. The anniversary of his landing in the Americas (Columbus Day) is celebrated throughout North and South America as well as in Spain and Italy.

Ten Things to Know by Heart

As a dad, you will sometimes have questions fired at you by schoolteachers, scoutmasters, or doctors that you just won't have the answers to, making you look like an idiot.

Here are some things you should know by heart about your child and some things you can settle for just knowing where to look them up.

1. Your child's full name — Duh . . .

2. Your child's date of birth — Again, duh . . .

3. Your child's allergies — You obviously don't want to feed a peanut to a child who is allergic to them.

4. Your child's current favorite food.

5. Your child's current favorite bedtime toy or story.

6. The name and phone number of your child's doctor.

7. Your child's current weight. This is very important when, at three in the morning, they have a fever and you need to know what the correct medicine dosage is.

8. What your child is wearing today. This is important in the scary but unlikely event that you need to describe your child to the police should he or she go missing.

9. What things scare your child.

10. Your child's best friends' names.

What's in the Attic?

There's nothing in the attic but spiders and dust and useless old junk, right? Wrong! Well, there may be plenty of spiders and dust but you can bet that old junk isn't all useless, it's a treasure trove! Crawling around in the musty room upstairs searching for hidden gems is worth the effort, unless you happen to live in an apartment complex, in which case the neighbors who live above might not be too pleased. But even if you don't have an attic, your parents probably do, and having a look around can bring back all sorts of memories from your childhood that you can share with your kids.

Here are our Top Ten finds that will have you reminiscing about the good old days — now get out that stepladder and see what you can find.

1. The train set or Legos that used to be your favorite toy, but you were only allowed to play with on special occasions because your mom didn't like it cluttering the house.

2. The bike you first learned to ride, hanging on for dear life as your dad pushed you down a hill so that you could "learn to balance."

3. The old family photographs that your mom used to bring out every so often to make you cringe, but now fill you with nostalgia.

4. The trophy you won playing for your junior high football team.

5 The piles and piles of schoolbooks that your mom hasn't thrown out yet . . . even though you finished school twenty years ago!

6 Your old Boy Scout uniform.

7 The comic books you now wished you had been more careful with because they'd be worth a fortune these days.

8 Your computer games that now make you feel old because you can see exactly how far technology has advanced.

9 The complete set of the Hardy Boys books that you loved reading as a boy. Give them to your kids, they will love them, too!

10 Your old vinyl (yes, remember vinyl?) albums and singles. In this digital age, how many people still have a turntable? If you do, then stick your records on and relive your youth!

Top Ten Gifts for Dads

If your offspring are stuck for present ideas, leave this book conveniently open to this page. Make sure you do this just before your birthday, Christmas, or Father's Day, or it'll be socks and underwear again!

1. New power drill
2. Motorized coin sorter
3. Flash drive key ring
4. New set of golf clubs
5. Flat-screen TV
6. Comfy slippers
7. New Porsche or BMW
8. Gift certificate to your favorite steakhouse
9. Washing your car and mowing the lawn
10. Taking you fishing

If your parents never had children,
chances are you won't either.
Dick Cavett

Dad's Dream Cars

Bored with driving your family minivan or station wagon? Why not sit back and take a little time to fantasize about the car you *really* want to be seen driving! Unless you're loaded, you're about as likely to get your hands on one of these dream machines as you are to win total control of the TV remote. One of the best things about them is most have absolutely no room for the kids.

Ferrari Enzo

You know it's never going to become a reality and that's why this tops the list. Ferarri only made 349 of these cars and, even if you'd just won the lottery, they decided who was worthy of buying them. The 6-liter V12 engine produces 660 bhp (brake horsepower), allowing you to go from 0 to 60 in 3.65 seconds. The Enzo has a top speed of 218 mph and even has a button that lifts the nose of the car up so you won't damage your pride and joy going over a speed bump.

Mercedes SLR McLaren

If you want to feel a bit like James Bond, then this is the car for you. You enter the SLR through beetle-wing doors and spark the car into action by flipping the top of the gear shift to expose the starter button. Its 5.5-liter V8 supercharged engine produces 626 bhp, going from 0 to 60 in 3.6 seconds, with a top speed of 208 mph. With a production run of 3,500, it is slightly more accessible than the Enzo, but the fact that anyone over six feet tall will find it almost impossible to drive may turn you off.

Lamborghini Murciélago

Lamborghini is a name synonymous with dream cars: Almost every boy has dreamed of driving one. The Murciélago is the latest to roll off the production line (if not trip off the tongue!) and is far more gentle on the wallet. The 6.2 liter V12 produces 575 bhp, does 0 to 60 in 3 seconds and reaches a top speed of 205 mph. There's a rear spoiler that automatically angles to 50 degrees at 81 mph and 70 degrees at 137 mph, by which time that police car will be just a dot in the rearview mirror!

Aston Martin Vantage

Unveiled at the 2005 Geneva Motor Show, the Vantage has been labeled the "must-have sports car." It's easy to see why when you look at the impressive performance figures: 0 to 60 in 4.9 seconds, with a top speed of 175 mph. How can you put a price on seeing your friends' faces when you say, "My other car's an Aston Martin"? But it is far more affordable than many of the cars featured here. With a V8 quad-cam 32-valve engine that is hand-assembled, this really is one of the ultimate muscle cars.

Porsche Carrera GT

Originally intended to dominate the Le Mans 24-hour race, rule changes made the Carrera GT ineligible so it was the driving public who benefited. Porsche has developed a 7-liter V10 engine that creates a monstrous 612 bhp and a top speed of 208 mph. It does 0 to 60 in 3.9 seconds and will take less than ten seconds to hit 124 mph. At only 46 inches high, it will look sleek in your driveway, even if you struggle to get in it!

Pagani Zonda F

Dedicated to the memory of legendary F1 driver Juan Manuel Fangio, the rearwheel drive Zonda F boasts a 7.3-liter V12 engine that produces more than 600 bhp. It flies to 60 mph in 3.6 seconds and will do over 210 mph flat-out. Futuristic carbon-fiber construction means it weighs about the same as a medium-size family hatchback, but that's where the comparison ends.

TVR Tuscan S

If you want a pure driving experience at a realistic budget, then save up for the TVR Tuscan S. Although it does boast an electrically assisted steering wheel and firmer suspension, it doesn't waste time with the needless niceties of traction control, antilock brakes, or airbags — an approach that allows the car to hit a very respectable 175 mph.

Lotus Sport Exige 240R

The Lotus name evokes images of sports cars that will transport you back to your childhood. The Exige 240R has a finely tuned 1.8-liter engine that produces 243 bhp and a top speed of 155 mph. With the ability to reach 60 mph in a very respectable 3.9 seconds, every father should have one for when he needs some quiet time on his own!

Ford GT

For those of you with a nostalgic side, the Ford GT's retro styling will suit you perfectly. It has a supercharged V8 engine that produces 550 bhp and a top speed of 205 mph. You'll be able to leave your rivals standing at the lights with an extremely impressive 0 to 60 time of 3.3 seconds. The trouble is that Ford is only going to manufacture 4,200 of these cars and demand will be high.

Hummer H2

If you have to imagine yourself in one car that can easily accommodate a family, then this is it. For those fathers who still have a yearning to play soldier, the military-styled Hummer H2 is the car for you. While not the perfect vehicle for running errands — it's enormous, and fuel efficiency diminishes to practically nothing when you put your foot down — a 16-inch wall will prove no obstacle for the H2. It's powered by a 6-liter V8 and labors to 60 mph in more than 10 seconds, but once you get up to a reasonable speed it's perfect for cruising the highways.

How to Teach Your Child to Dive

There's nothing more flashy than a perfectly executed, graceful dive into the swimming pool, and nothing more embarrassing than a painful belly flop that sprays everyone with water. Make sure you are capable of the graceful version before you start trying to teach your child to dive.

You must also make sure that the pool is suitable for diving. Be very careful and make sure there are no NO DIVING signs posted — hitting the bottom can cause serious injuries.

So, providing that you are sure that the pool, or the sea, if you are diving off a jetty or rock, is deep enough, you can try showing your youngster how it's done. Once they are confident swimmers, kids love jumping into pools or the sea, and it comes quite naturally to them. Diving, however, is something that can take a while to master. Going in headfirst is not as simple as hitting the water butt first. Children have to be good swimmers before trying this, though, because they should never dive while wearing any kind of flotation device or any encumbrances such as face masks or snorkels. Regular swimming goggles are okay.

Show How it's Done

The first thing to do is to demonstrate your dive. Make sure that you show them how to stand at the edge of the pool properly. Your toes should be able to curl over the edge, and your balance should be on the balls of your feet. Then bend your knees and lean forward from the waist, duck your head down,

and bring your arms up so that your hands will hit the water first.

Spring off the side and straighten your legs behind you. After hitting the water, push your head back and arch your back so that you swoop up to the surface still facing away from the side of the pool.

The Forward Roll

Your child can't be expected to get all of that right the first time, so start him or her off from a crouched position so that he or she can "roll" forward into the water. Make sure that your pupil straightens up in the water, though, because you don't want him or her to do a complete forward roll and risk banging his or her head against the side. You should be in the water supervising this to make sure that does not happen. When performing this "roll," the arms should still be held out in front of the head to break the water first.

From the crouch, you can progress to standing slightly more erect, always ensuring that your pupil achieves a "swoop" in the water to take him or her away from the edge.

Now you need to encourage the flexing of the knees to give a little spring to the dive and force the legs up behind. You should tell your child to try to arc like a rainbow through the air and imagine a square patch on the surface of the water that he or she should aim to hit with his or her hands.

With some practice, a child who is already comfortable with jumping in and swimming will soon master the dive and, doubtless, be telling *you* where you're going wrong.

Children really brighten up a household —
they never turn the lights off.
Ralph Bus

Dads on the Sideline

When your son or daughter starts taking part in competitive sports, whether it be tennis, football, soccer, hockey, basketball, lacrosse, or any other team sport, you will be expected not only to take your child to and from games, but also to show the proper kind of support during the game.

Your child will appreciate your presence, but not if you make a complete fool of yourself, so don't embarrass him or her by getting overexcited. Here are a few dos and don'ts for attending your offspring's sporting events:

1. Do bring an umbrella if you're going to be outside. Obviously an umbrella is going to look pretty stupid at an indoor basketball or volleyball game.

2. Don't question the referee's parentage.

3. Do applaud the team, not just your own child. Your youngster wants to be part of the team, not constantly singled out by a bawling father.

4. Don't shout, "Break his leg, son!"

5. Do stand away from the action to avoid flying balls/players. Your child does not want to have to take an injured parent to the hospital after the game.

6. Don't make loud comments about the manager or coach's IQ if he or she keeps your child on the bench.

7. Do stand with other parents of children on your son's or daughter's team, and don't get into a fracas with the opposition's parents.

8 Don't hug any of the other parents present.

9 Do stress the values of the game. Play to win, but play with respect and if you don't win, be a good sport.

10 Don't run onto the field and join in the goal celebrations.

The Joke's on You

Fathers are expected to come out with some cheesy lines. So here are a few to get you going. In fact, you may have heard a few of these yourself from your own dad!

✱

Whenever you come home from work and sit at an empty plate, flip your tie onto it and say, "I don't know about you, but I'm having Thai tonight."

✱

Playfully (and gently!) boot your boy's backside, and when he turns around with a look of indignation, say, "Nice to see I can still make an impression."

✱

At the New Year's Eve party, it's two minutes past midnight and you say, "I haven't had a drink all year."

✱

When there's fruit on the table and you're asked if you'd like a pear, you always say, "No thanks, just one will do."

✱

When someone coughs, you say, "It's not the cough that carries you off, it's the coffin they carry you off in."

✱

When you are asked to put on your kid's shoes, you say, "But they won't fit me."

Whenever you hear the name Isabelle mentioned,
you say, "Isabelle necessary on a bike?"

Whenever you hear the name Mary mentioned,
you say, "Ho-ho-ho . . . Mary Christmas."

When asked to pay for something or dish out the
allowance, you pull some bills from your wallet and
say, "But these are my favorite steak vouchers."

When that tie box is handed to you at Christmas,
you say, "Don't tell me . . . it's a book."

Whenever you are asked if you are having trouble hearing,
you say, "Eh?"

If you are caught talking to yourself, you say, "It's the only
way I can get a decent conversation around here."

✱

When your child wants something to eat and says,
"I'm hungry," you say, "I'm Germany, pleased to meet you."

✱

When driving past some black-and-white cows, you say, "Boy,
it must be cold out there . . . those cows are Friesian!"

✱

At dinner, when the meat is placed in front of you to carve, you say, "Well, here's my dinner . . . what are the rest of you going to eat?"

✱

On a car trip when you are asked, "Where are we, Dad?" you say, "In the car."

✱

Whenever you are offered a doughnut, you sing, "Doughnut forsake me, oh, my darling . . ."

✱

When your child wants something to drink and says, "I'm thirsty," you say, "Hi, I'm Friday!"

✱

If your partner asks you to put the kettle on, you say, "I don't think it will fit."

✱

If you are asked to "put the cat out," you say, "I didn't realize it was on fire."

✱

When you are asked if you caught the train/bus, you say, "No, my net wasn't big enough."

✱

Should someone ever ask, "Where's the paper?" you say, "In the kitchen cabinet beside the salt."

Whenever you take off your shoes, you wiggle them
in front of your face, sing some nonsense, and say,
"That's sole music for you."

Upon hearing someone in a restaurant dropping glasses
or dishes, you say, "Fire the juggler!" or "That's smashing!"
or, like Long John Silver's parrot, "Pieces of plate!
Pieces of plate!"

On entering anywhere that has stuffed and mounted animal
heads on display, you say, "It must have been going pretty fast
to come straight through that wall!"

At a Greek restaurant, the waiter hands you the menu,
and you say, "Can you recommend something?
This menu's all Greek to me."

The waiter mentions one of the specials tonight is chicken,
and you say, "None for me . . . it's foul!"

When being offered a hot towel in a Japanese restaurant,
you say, "No thank you, I'm full!"

The waiter recommends the duck and you say,
"As long as I don't get the bill."

✻

When eating mushrooms, you must always say,
"I'd like to eat more, but I don't have mush room."

✻

When any child puts ketchup on his or her plate, you say,
"Do you want some food to go with your ketchup?"

✻

After a large meal, you say, "Well that was a nice starter,
now what's for dinner?"

✻

When a child asks, "May I please leave the table?" you say,
"Well, you weren't thinking of taking it with you, were you?"

✻

After a meal you say, "Good thing we ate when we did,
because I'm not hungry now."

✻

If your child moans, "Well, it's just not fair!" you say,
"Well, it's just not raining . . ."

✻

When you are asked, "Is it Wednesday today?"
you say, "All day . . ."

✻

If a child asks, "Dad, can you put my shirt on?" you say,
"Sure, I can put it on the dog."

When anyone asks, "Can you call me a taxi?" you say,
"Of course . . . you're a taxi."

When a child is poking around in his or her ear, you say,
"Never put anything in your ear sharper than your elbow."

If you are asked, "Dad, can you pick me up tonight?"
you say, "As long as you don't put on any more weight."

When Mom says, "Can you make me a cup of coffee?"
you wave your hand over her head and say,
"Abracadabra! You are now a cup of coffee."

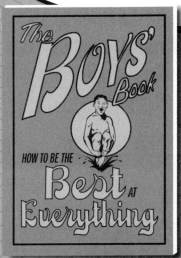
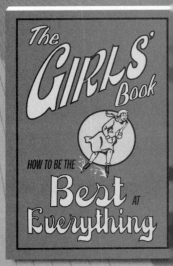